DIVINE PERSPECTIVES

A 40-Day Journey to Discover Christ's

Vision for You in Your Church.

Copyright © 2023

Narrow Gate Missions
Ministerio Vida Plena

Narrow Gate
Missions   **VIDA PLENA**

ISBN: 9798877225084

Lord Teach us to Pray

Luke 11:1

Week One

Day 1

Avoid the Tragedy of Unbelief

Read Matthew 13:53-58

> *"And He did not do many miracles there because of their unbelief." Matthew 13:58 (HCSB)*

In the radiant light of the glorious embrace of the Spirit, let us delve into this passage, which is undoubtedly one of the most poignant in the sacred pages of the Bible. It narrates the poignant moment when our Savior, Jesus Christ, returned to His very own hometown to impart His divine wisdom and grace to the eager ears of His fellow townspeople.

As His celestial words flowed forth, a sense of awe and astonishment gripped those fortunate souls who were present. The depth of His wisdom and the power of His teachings left them spellbound. However, as we peer into the hearts of those who heard Him, we are met with a heavy lament. For their astonishment, though genuine, failed to stir within them the flames of obedience and faith that should have ignited their souls.

Oh, the potential that lay dormant within their lives! A potential for radical transformation, a potential for the betterment of their community, all lay at their feet like precious gems waiting to be unearthed. Yet,

3

alas, no positive changes graced the people of Nazareth or their beloved town. Why, you may ask? The Scriptures provide us with a profound answer - *"Because of their unbelief."*

Let us pause and reflect on the gravity of those words. Unbelief, that cold and formidable barrier, stood resolute, shutting the door to the transformative power of our Lord and Savior, Jesus Christ. It is faith, the fervent belief in His omnipotent grace, that swings wide open the floodgates to that very same transformational power.

In contrast to the story of Nazareth, the Bible is full of stories about Jesus doing amazing things because people had faith in him. *(See Matthew 9:2; 9:22; 15:28; Mark 10:52; Luke 8:48)*

When our Lord casts His loving eyes upon your life, what does He perceive? Does He find an attitude of unwavering faith, steadfast and resolute? Or does He encounter the shadow of unbelief, lingering in the recesses of your heart?

Do you firmly believe, with all the passion of your spirit, that Jesus can perform a miraculous work within your church? Do you hold fast to the unwavering belief that He will, in His divine wisdom and timing, breathe new life into the body of believers? Do you recognize that your faithful attendance at the house of the Lord and your fervent prayers for His divine intervention in your church play pivotal roles in this glorious process?

Let these questions resonate in the depths of your soul, for in them lie the keys to unlocking the transformative power of our Lord, Jesus Christ. May your faith be unwavering, and may His grace flood your hearts, your churches, and your communities.

Prayer

If your unbelief is a roadblock to Jesus working in your life and in your church, confess the sin of unbelief. Ask God to strengthen your faith in Him. (Mark 9:24)

Day 2

Remember God's Power

Read Jeremiah 32:17-44

> *"Ah, Lord God! You Yourself made the heavens and earth by Your great power and with Your outstretched arm. Nothing is too difficult for You!"* Jeremiah 32:17 (HCSB)

Take a moment to remember how powerful our Almighty God is. Though life is full of problems and difficulties, it is all too easy to lose sight of how great He is. We let our problems throw a shadow over the beauty of our Creator without meaning to, and when we do, we make God seem weak and helpless.

Let us go on a trip to renew our faith in our Heavenly Father's power. The prophet Jeremiah tells us to think about the amazing things God has done in the past to remember how powerful He is. Because it was He who, in the beginning, spoke and the stars and the earth came into being. Wow, what an amazing display of divine power! When God spoke, the universe exploded in all its glory. Really, only God could do something so amazing. The very act of creation shows that God can do anything.

Yet, creation is just the opening act in the grand symphony of God's mighty works. Jeremiah compels us to remember that this same God, with signs and wonders, led His people out of the bondage of Egypt

(v. 21). Every Sunday morning, as we gather in His presence, and as we immerse ourselves in the Scriptures during our devotional time, we are reminded that this very God sent His only begotten Son, Jesus Christ. Born of a virgin, He walked this earth sinless, willingly laid down His life on a cross to bear the weight of our sins, and triumphantly rose from the grave on the third day. Such an astonishing feat can only be attributed to God's boundless might. The death, burial, and resurrection of Jesus Christ stand as an indomitable reminder that our God is capable of the extraordinary.

Perhaps you have forgotten that God is able to do anything. Now is a good time to remember all the amazing things God has done, as told in the Bible. Take a moment to think about the wonderful things He has done in each of our lives. We should also be proud of the amazing things He has done inside the walls of our buildings. That is because these memories will help us have new faith, fresh feelings, and hearts full of the unwavering belief that our God can do anything.

Prayer

Ask God to do a work of revitalization in your church that only He can get credit for.

Day 3

Confess Pride/Embrace Humility

Read Luke 18:9-14

> *"I tell you, this one went down to his house justified rather than the other; because everyone who exalts himself will be humbled, but the one who humbles himself will be exalted."* Luke 18:14 (HCSB)

Let us delve into the depths of a profound truth. Pride is a sin that often lurks in the shadows, eluding our awareness. It is a cunning adversary, not easily discerned within the confines of our own hearts. Our Lord and Savior, Jesus Christ, in His infinite wisdom, presented us with a parable that vividly illustrates the stark contrast between pride and humility, two diametrically opposed forces that shape the fabric of our souls.

In this story, there are two different people, each of whom is the opposite of the other. The tax collector, who is a humble person, is the essence of humility, while the Pharisee, who is well-known, is the essence of pride.

Pride is characterized by an unwillingness to acknowledge one's own need. Not once in the parable does the Pharisee concede his need for divine intervention. Conversely, humility readily recognizes its own insufficiency. The tax collector, in an act of utter humility, strikes his chest and acknowledges his desperate need for forgiveness, confessing his sinfulness before the Almighty.

Pride, with its arrogant demeanor, possesses a keen eye for the faults of others. The Pharisee proudly proclaims, *"I thank you that I am not like those other people who are greedy, unrighteous adulterers."* In stark contrast, humility, with its tender heart, gazes inward, acknowledging its own transgressions. The tax collector humbly implores, *"God, turn your wrath from me, a sinner."*

The paramount concern of pride revolves around the perceptions of others, as it seeks validation and approval from the world. The Pharisee, in his prayer, boasts of his own accomplishments, proclaiming, *"I fast twice a week, I give a tenth of everything I get."* Conversely, humility's primary focus is on the opinion of God. It yearns for His favor and seeks to align itself with His divine will.

Let us take this sacred lesson to heart. May we be vigilant against the stealthy presence of pride in our lives, ever ready to acknowledge our need for God's grace. Let us adopt the posture of humility, recognizing our own shortcomings and seeking God's mercy above all else. For it is in humility that we find favor in the eyes of the Almighty, and it is in His approval that our hearts truly rejoice. May our lives be a testament to the transformational power of humility, to the glory of our Lord and Savior, Jesus Christ.

Prayer

Pray that God revive love for church and his Word and that He will reveal any areas of unhealthy pride in your life and show you His way to true humility.

Day 4

Purify Your Heart

"The pure in heart are blessed, for they will see God." Matthew 5:8 (HCSB)

In the heart of Vancouver, Washington, a place where snowflakes would gently descend from the heavens, I found immense joy in standing amidst the falling snow, watching it blanket the world in a pristine white embrace. However as beautiful as this snow may be, it bears a lesson about the world we inhabit. The snow quickly picks up the dirty things from the world around it, which is a shame. As cars from around the world drive on it, the otherwise perfect white cloth gets scratched up and turns a sad brown.

In the teachings of our Lord and Savior, Jesus Christ, we uncover a profound truth - the blessedness of the pure in heart. To glimpse the divine presence of our Almighty God is a promise of unparalleled magnitude. But I urge you to think about a very important question: When was the last time you saw God's face? So, the wonder of God's presence will stay out of reach until our hearts are purified.Satan, our enemy, is very smart, so he does not mind if our thoughts stay full of worldly things. So, even though our hearts are spiritually pure, they can look like snow that has lost its shine because of the stain of this world.

In this passage of God's Word, we find a magnificent promise linked to the purity of heart - the promise of beholding God Himself. To witness the Almighty amidst the darkness of our sinful world serves to refine the purity of our hearts. Please think about the state of your heart as you think about this verse today. Is it clean, free from the reach of this world? Are your goals to catch a glimpse of the God who makes hearts pure? On the other hand, have the vibrant hues of this world dimmed the pristine presence of God within you?

To witness the marvelous work of God in the midst of your local church family necessitates individuals who are wholly devoted and possess hearts purified by the Holy Spirit. Let us unite in fervent prayer for the precious members of our congregation who exemplify the purity of heart we aspire to attain. May their unwavering devotion inspire us all to strive for a heart that remains untarnished by the world's impurities, that we may behold our Lord and Savior in His full glory.

Prayer

God, show me today the dirty parts of my heart and give me the strength to give them to you to clean up. Please give me the drive to keep my heart pure.

Day 5

Search Me, O God

Read Psalm 139:23-24

"Search me, God, and know my heart; test me and know my concerns." Psalm 139:23 (HCSB)

It's not just about asking the Lord for material blessings like a larger house, a newer car, a ministry promotion, or a salary increase. It's about reaching out to the Almighty God, the God of Abraham, Isaac, and Jacob, and inviting Him to search our hearts and test our thoughts. The Bible teaches us that God is all-knowing, all-powerful, and ever-present. Truly, His awareness of us beyond our own understanding. He has knowledge of both real occurrences and potential outcomes that are unlikely to occur. Our Heavenly Father is never taken off guard.

In the world of healthcare, professionals advise us to undergo regular physical checkups to maintain our well-being. Early detection of any health issues is crucial for a long and healthy life. Just as we prioritize our physical health, it's equally important to pay attention to our spiritual well-being. Thus, we set aside a special time, free from our daily duties and tasks, to closely examine our Christian journey. We long for those moments of solitude with the One who knows us intimately. When we find ourselves alone with God, we earnestly request Him to peer into the depths of our hearts and minds. Are we still deeply in love with Jesus, as we once were? Have we allowed trivial matters to keep us from attending church? Are we at times merely going through the motions, offering lip service rather than genuine worship? Can we honestly say that we cherish our church family? Are we teetering on the edge of spiritual compromise? In these moments of introspection, we ask ourselves whether our hearts are filled with humility or pride.

Being in the presence of God and being completely honest with Him can bring about a refreshing renewal of our spirits. Statistics show that a revived believer often serves as the catalyst for a church's revival. So, when was the last time you underwent a spiritual examination?

Step aside and let God reexamine your heart and life. Personal rebirth can spark church and communal revival. Let us connect with God and make our love for Jesus stronger than before.

Prayer

Consider making a decision, setting a date, securing a place, and practicing a time of solitude with God. With an open Bible and blank pieces of paper, ask God to search your heart and attitude.

Day 6

He Must Become Greater

Read John 3:30

> *"He must increase, but I must decrease."* John 3:30 (HCSB)

In the realm of Christian living, we must always remain vigilant, for it is not immune to dangers. The enemy loves it when Christians stray from God's way, causing fights in churches and tearing down ministries. One of the enemy's most potent weapons is the poison of pride. As we find in Proverbs 16:18, *"Pride comes before destruction, and an arrogant spirit before a fall."*

Let us take the example of John the Baptist, whose heart was pure and focused on the Son of God, the Savior of the world. John's ultimate desire was for people to fix their gaze upon Jesus, not upon himself. He yearned for the world to remember the name of Jesus, the One who deserves all glory and honor.

The trouble arises when Christians deviate from the path that John set. A prideful churchgoer may start to believe that the spotlight should be on them, positioning themselves to climb the so-called "social ladder" of Christian success. They may even seek credit for the growth and advancement of the

15

church. But it is God's desire for His Son to increase and for His servants to decrease. Jesus should be the central thread woven into every sermon and Bible study, receiving the glory and honor that rightfully belong to Him. His grace must be embraced and shared, and His guidance followed with wholehearted devotion and surrender.

Take a moment to reflect upon your own life. Are you following the inspirational example set by John the Baptist? Is the spotlight shining upon you, or is it illuminating the One who transformed and called you? Let us strive to emulate John's humility and devotion, ensuring that Jesus Christ remains the focus of our lives and ministries. In doing so, we honor the One who is truly worthy of all praise and worship.

Prayer

If Jesus is increasing, praise the Father. If you're increasing, repent and experience a new beginning.

Day 7

Read Matthew 13:1-9

"Still others fell on good ground and produced a crop: some 100, some 60, and some 30 times what was sown." Matthew 13:8 (HCSB)

Jesus addressed a vast assembly with a parable, a spiritual message woven into a story from our earthly realm. He chose this method to delve into the very core of a person's heart. In His teaching, He spoke of different types of soil: good soil, rough ground, thorny ground, and even soil along the road. The purpose was to convey the importance of having hearts capable of yielding a bountiful harvest.

So, let us ponder the state of our hearts at this moment. In Jesus' parable, He vividly portrays four kinds of soil, which symbolize the conditions of our hearts:

The Calloused Heart: This heart lacks spiritual expectancy, often going through religious motions and approaching God with selfish motives.

The Shallow Heart: This heart may be immature in faith and too preoccupied with worldly matters to fully serve. It's akin to

17

being broad in appearance but lacking depth in spirituality.

The Distracted Heart: This heart struggles with the worries of life and the draw of money or family, which takes its attention away from God's plans.

The Productive Heart: This heart is dedicated to living a life that fulfills God's mission. Just as one must break the ground (soil) to plant a garden, so too must our hearts undergo a process of brokenness to yield a spiritual harvest. It is often through brokenness that God accomplishes His work in us.

Are you willing to be broken for the glory of God? What is currently breaking your heart and spirit? Reflect upon the condition of your heart today. What type of soil represents your heart at this moment? Let us earnestly seek the transformation of our hearts, so they may be fertile ground for the seeds of God's Word and His divine purpose.

Self-Examination

The Christian must perceive his or her own wickedness in light of God's perspective....

"Create in me a clean heart, O God, and renew a steadfast spirit within me. Do not cast me away from Thy presence and do not take Thy Holy Spirit from me. Restore to me the joy of Thy salvation, and sustain me with a willing spirit." Psalm 51:10-12

1. **Creating a Clean Heart:** As we approach God in prayer, we recognize the need for a heart transformation. We invite the Holy Spirit to create within us a heart that is pure, free from the stains of sin. We understand that the Holy Spirit is the agent of change, cleansing us from within and making us new creations in Christ.

2. **Renewing a Steadfast Spirit:** Our journey with God necessitates a persistent and unshakeable spirit. We ask the Holy Spirit to make us stronger in our faith and our love for Jesus and his Church. We can trust the Spirit is strength to help us stand strong in the face of trials and challenges because of this renewal. Lacking the power that comes from the Holy Spirit, many leave the church.

3. **Abiding in God's Presence:** We acknowledge the importance of God's presence in our lives. The Holy Spirit is our constant companion,

and we pray that we may never be separated from Him. Our faith and faithfulness emphasizes the ongoing relationship with the Spirit, knowing that His presence sustains us.

4. **The Joy of Salvation:** The joy of our salvation is a precious gift from God. We seek the restoration of this joy, knowing that it is the Spirit's work to revive our spirits and fill us with unspeakable joy. We often experience the joy of the Lord as we yield to the Spirit's leading and in our faithfulness to the house of the Lord.

5. **Upheld by the Generous Spirit:** We depend on the Holy Spirit's generosity to support us on our journey of faith. His generous Spirit upholds us, guides us, and empowers us to live victorious lives as charismatic believers.

The Holy Spirit's transforming power is something we wholeheartedly embrace as Spirit-led believers. Psalm 51:10-12 serves as a powerful prayer that reflects our desire for a clean heart, a steadfast spirit, God's abiding presence, the joy of salvation, and the sustaining power of the Holy Spirit. May we continually seek this transformation and experience the abundant life that the Spirit offers. We ask that His Spirit nourish our hearts today, infuse us with a passion for serving others, and pour out His presence in a new way.

grace

Week Two

Day 8

Ask, Seek, and Knock

Read Matthew 7:7-12

> *"Keep asking, and it will be given to you. Keep searching, and you will find. Keep knocking, and the door will be opened to you."* Matthew 7:7 (HCSB)

The Word of God shines brightly, illuminating the undeniable truth that our Heavenly Father responds with great fervor to the passionate supplications of His devoted children, aligning His divine will with the revival and restoration of His beloved church. It is incumbent upon us to recognize that the delay in experiencing this revival may be a result of our prematurely relinquishing our prayers.

Consider a tender moment when a little girl observed her mother applying a layer of cold cream to her face. Innocently, the child inquired, "Mommy, what is the purpose of this act?" With grace, the mother responded, "My dear, I do this to enhance my beauty." As the mother began to wipe away the cream after a brief pause, the curious child questioned, "Are you giving up already?"

In our pursuit of spiritual growth, we must take this lesson to heart. Let us resolve to never abandon our prayers prematurely. Instead, let our petitions be offered to the Almighty with unwavering persistence and fervency. The very verbs "ask, seek, and knock" are imbued with a sense of unceasing, continuous action. In essence, Jesus imparts the profound message, "Ask, and keep on asking. Seek, and keep on seeking. Knock, and keep on knocking."

Do you pray regularly and deeply for the holy fire to shine again in your church? If your church is hungry for rebirth, I beg you, dear brothers and sisters, to stand firm in your prayerful efforts until you hear from heaven. Embrace the command of our Lord with unwavering faith: Ask, seek, and knock!

Prayer

Begin your journey of ongoing, fervent prayer for your church's revitalization today. God will answer in His time.

Day 9

Value His Name

"Samuel replied, "Don't be afraid. Even though you have committed all this evil, don't turn away from following the LORD. Instead, worship the LORD with all your heart. Don't turn away to follow worthless things that can't profit or deliver you; they are worthless. The LORD will not abandon His people, because of His great name and because He has determined to make you His own people." 1 Samuel 12:20-22 (HCSB)

Over the course of the past decade, we've witnessed fluctuations in the worth of many earthly possessions—houses, retirement funds, salaries, and more. These changes have had profound and lasting impacts on both individuals and businesses. Indeed, value in the material realm is an ever-shifting phenomenon. But what if I were to tell you that there exists something of incomprehensible and unchanging value? A treasure so divine, it remains eternally priceless. We are blessed to possess a Savior whose worth transcends all earthly measures!

Turning our hearts to the verses of 1 Samuel, we are reminded that even in moments when we have strayed from the path of righteousness, we must never turn away from our Lord. For the name of the Lord holds immeasurable value for us. It is in the very nature of our God that He shall never forsake His people. It is not because we possess great intrinsic value, but rather, it is due to the inestimable worth of His holy name and His impeccable reputation.

Pause and ponder, do you truly perceive the unfathomable value inherent in the name of the LORD? And as you examine the tapestry of your life, does it radiate the depth of the worth you ascribe to our Lord?

Let us, as devout believers, be ever vigilant to recognize and embrace the eternal value of the name of our precious LORD, and let our lives resound with the testimony of this priceless truth.

Prayer

Pray today that the value of God's name would be seen in your life so that a world may see HIM. Pray that your church would reflect the value of the name of the LORD.

Day 10

Bear the Fruit of the Holy Spirit

Read Galatians 5:22-26

> *"But the fruit of the Spirit is love, joy, peace, longsuffering, gentleness, goodness, faith, meekness, temperance: against such there is no law."* Galatians 5:22-23 (NIV)

As devoted disciples of our Lord Jesus Christ, we are called to surrender ourselves daily to the divine guidance of the Holy Spirit. In the sacred words of verse 25, we are admonished to "live by the Spirit" and "follow the Spirit." The unmistakable sign that the Holy Spirit is at the helm of our lives is the manifestation of spiritual fruit.

Just as a ripe apple serves as the visible testimony to the inner reality of an apple tree, so does the fruit of the Holy Spirit serve as the outward testament to the Holy Spirit's sovereign leadership in our lives.

When we wholeheartedly yield to the gentle promptings of the Holy Spirit, our existence becomes adorned with the exquisite virtues of love, joy, peace, patience, kindness, faithfulness, gentleness, and self-control. It is the divine intention of our Heavenly Father to cultivate these virtues within us as we submit ourselves to His divine guidance. Conversely, when the Holy Spirit is not the guiding force in our lives, we may find ourselves lacking in love, devoid of joy, restless, impatient, unkind, and surrendering to chaos.

Imagine, if the person who knows you most intimately were to employ the qualities listed in verses 22 and 23 as a measure of your character. How would they describe you? Would they testify to your boundless love, your abiding joy, your unswerving patience, and your gentle kindness? Let us ponder these questions and aspire to be living testimonies of the Holy Spirit's transformative power within us.

Prayer

Yield today to the work of the Holy Spirit in you. Ask God to produce in you the fruit of His Holy Spirit.

Day 11

Forfeit My Agenda

Read Luke 22:39-46

"Father, if You are willing, take this cup away from Me — nevertheless, not My will, but Yours, be done." Luke 22:42 (HCSB)

In contemplating the profound mystery of our Lord and Savior, Jesus Christ, we are reminded that He was both fully divine and fully human. In the passage before us, we are granted a glimpse into the humanity of Jesus, where He grapples with the divine will of the Father in the face of His impending suffering and sacrificial death. Jesus, in His perfect humanity, was acutely aware that within a few fleeting hours, He would bear the weight of the world's sin upon His shoulders. The Holy Scriptures declare, *"He who knew no sin became sin for us, that we might become the righteousness of God in Him."*

We observe a passionate and powerful prayer that goes beyond the limits of common petition when we find Jesus in the garden of Gethsemane. His anguish was so profound that His very sweat resembled drops of blood falling to the ground (verse 44). On one hand, the Savior's heart longed for the Father to remove the cup of suffering from His path. Yet, in the depth of His soul, He comprehended that

29

this very suffering and sacrificial death were indispensable for the salvation of precious souls and the fulfillment of the Father's divine plan for His life. Thus, at the height of His unity with the Father, He bowed down to the divine plan, saying, *"Not my will but Yours be done."*

Above all else, Jesus' heart yearned for the Father's will to be fulfilled in His life, for it was the heartbeat of His divine mission and the salvation of humanity that rested upon this profound surrender to the Father's perfect plan.

Prayer

Today, ask God to help you surrender your will, your preferences, and your agenda so that you may fulfill his purpose for your life in his church. Put your trust in God's plan, just like Jesus did.

Day 12

Live According To The Spirit

Read Romans 8:5-8

"For those who live according to the flesh think about the things of the flesh, but those who live according to the Spirit, about the things of the Spirit." Romans 8:5 (HCSB)

I love nothing more than relaxing up on my couch with my smart TV remote in hand, perusing the channels in search of the ideal film to lose myself in. This remarkable remote, adorned with a multitude of buttons, grants me access to various streaming applications, including the likes of Netflix, Hulu, and YouTube. Unfortunately, there are times when I am watching a streaming video and accidentally hit a button, which leads to an unexpected transition to a different streaming service. It takes me a brief moment of realization to discern that I have, by chance, pressed the wrong button.

In the sacred words of Romans 8:5, we are reminded of the inherent human struggle with sinful desires. It is a stark reality that we are born into a world where the allure of sin is all too pervasive, and thus, it should come as no surprise that we are inclined toward sinful inclinations. However, the text also underscores that those who walk in step with the Spirit respond in a manner that aligns with the spiritual nature. Our daily responses to life's circumstances serve as a vivid indicator of which nature is dominant within us: our sinful nature or our spiritual nature.

We stand at a crossroads, confronted with two distinct paths—the path of sin and the path of the Spirit. Regrettably, we often find ourselves speaking thoughtlessly and making hasty choices without due consideration, inadvertently choosing the wrong path.

Consider what transformation could unfold in your life if you consciously embraced your spiritual side each day? Reflect upon your congregation, your church family, and envision the impact of collectively nurturing our spiritual lives. I implore you to seek divine guidance, beseech the Lord to speak to your heart, and earnestly seek ways to cultivate your spiritual walk, setting forth a compelling example within your church community in the coming weeks.

Prayer

Pray God will show you areas of your life you need to allow Him to control. Also, pray for the leaders in your church to be guided by Him.

Day 13

Forgive One Another

Read Ephesians 4:25-32

"And be kind and compassionate to one another, forgiving one another, just as God also forgave you in Christ." Ephesians 4:32 (HCSB)

One universal truth that binds us all together is the experience of being wounded by others. Each of us, at some point, has endured the pain inflicted by hurtful words or actions. Sometimes, the deepest wounds stem from what someone failed to say or do. Life, it seems, does not ask whether we will be wounded, but rather, how we will choose to respond when others cause us pain.

The verses before us today unveils several common reactions that often accompany the wounds we endure: anger (verse 26), bitterness, wrath, malice (verse 31). When we recognize these destructive emotions festering within us, we are challenged to take decisive action—to "remove" or "put away" these toxic responses. Instead, we are beckoned to embrace the divine response of forgiveness.

Forgiveness is the very essence of God's divine relationship with us. It is the sacred path our Heavenly Father calls us to walk as we navigate our relationships with one another. In its purest form, forgiveness means treating the one who has hurt us as if their transgressions had never occurred. It entails the deliberate rejection of anger and bitterness in our interactions with them, and it beckons us to bestow grace upon the very individuals who have caused us pain.

Have you found yourself harboring anger, bitterness, wrath, or malice towards a fellow member of your church? I implore you, in this moment, to humbly confess these sinful responses before the Lord. Seek His divine assistance and rely upon His abundant grace to empower you to extend forgiveness to that person.

Let us, as devoted believers, be bearers of the divine gift of forgiveness, exemplifying the love and mercy of our Lord in our interactions with one another.

Prayer

Ask God to identify the presence of unforgiveness in your life. Confess the sin of unforgiveness. Ask God to produce in your life a humility that honors Him.

Day 14

Raise Up New Leaders

Read 2 Timothy 2:1-2

> *"And what you have heard from me in the presence of many witnesses, commit to faithful men who will be able to teach others also."*
> 2 Timothy 2:2 (HCSB)

Within the hallowed halls of our dear church, the faithful are echoing a single, powerful cry: bring forth more leaders. We pray that people will rise up and take charge in many areas of our church. We yearn for leaders to guide the children's programs, to shepherd the youth, to engage in outreach endeavors, and to contribute financially to the church's noble mission. Indeed, the need for leaders is vast and multifaceted.

But, have you ever paused to ponder where these leaders shall emerge from? Unless they relocate to our community or transfer from other congregations, the pool of potential leaders may seem limited. However, the wisdom of Paul, imparted to Timothy, holds the answer to this pressing concern—it is through raising up leaders from within our own midst.

Christian leaders are not born; they are shaped and molded through the transformative work of the Holy

Spirit. Finding deep direction in 2 Timothy 2:2 shows us how to raise up these leaders. It beckons mature Christian leaders to engage in the sacred duty of teaching and training faithful individuals who possess the potential to become leaders themselves. This, in turn, sets in motion a divine cascade as these new leaders are equipped to teach and train others in a continuous cycle of growth and discipleship.

So, I want you to think about this question: Are you ready to go through the training and preparing process so that you can eventually become a leader in your local church? The call to leadership is more than just a request to help out. It is an offer to be a part of the holy work that will shape the future of our community and further the Kingdom of our Lord.

Prayer

Please pray today that God will give you a vision and a plan for developing new leaders from within the church family.

Spiritual Renewal Begins with Me:

Embracing the Power of Small Groups for Spiritual Investment

The editorial of the Assemblies of God, known as "Gospel Publishing," has acknowledged the significant findings of Bible Study data and issued a profound statement. According to these findings, the key to achieving spiritual maturity is via the conscious and intentional decisions made by followers in their spiritual journey. In this framework, we acknowledge the crucial importance of Family Bible Studies and Small Groups as essential components in a disciple's deliberate strategy for spiritual rejuvenation.

Just as an ember, once separated from the fiery blaze, flickers and fades, so does our spiritual progress diminish when we distance ourselves from the fellowship of fellow believers. The essence of spiritual renewal and advancement necessitates a deeper engagement with the Family Bible Study or Small Group experience, extending beyond mere attendance. Here, we present ten transformative actions that can elevate your level of investment within your group, propelling you toward spiritual renewal and progress.

1. Seek God diligently through the study of His Word, both within the confines of your class

and during your daily quiet time.
2. Engage in fervent prayer, interceding for your group and actively inviting guests to join your class or group sessions.
3. Participate in open communication with your fellow group members.
4. Self-Cultivate a spirit of fellowship, both with your group members and with any guests who may join your gatherings.
5. Extend your hand to assist fellow group members in times of need, demonstrating Christ-like compassion and support.
6. Dedicate time pre-read and prepare to participate in class or group sessions, ensuring a spirit of receptivity and readiness.
7. Engage in class or group sessions with honesty and an open heart, contributing to the collective spiritual growth of the group.
8. Embrace a lifestyle that reflects the truths learned within your class or group sessions, allowing your faith to shine brightly in your daily walk.
9. Contribute your gifts and talents to serve the group and strengthen the church, contributing to unity and growth.
10. Wholeheartedly support initiatives aimed at equipping new leaders and establishing new groups, recognizing the value of multiplying the impact of your faith community.

As you reflect upon these transformative actions, take a moment to assess your commitment in each area, rating yourself from 1 to 10, with 1 signifying a weaker commitment and 10 representing a strong dedication. Identify the areas where you can be more intentional in supporting your spiritual growth and your group's growth. Ask God to guide you and involve your Pastor to encourage and support you in taking deliberate steps in the forthcoming month.

And if, by chance, you find yourself not yet part of a group, let this moment be an intentional step of spiritual renewal and growth. Seize the opportunity to join a group this week, for it is within the fellowship of believers that your faith shall be nurtured, your spirit renewed, and your journey of spiritual growth illuminated.

Week Three

Day 15

Teach Me to Love

Read I Thessalonians 4:9-12

> *"About brotherly love: You don't need me to write you because you yourselves are taught by God to love one another."* 1 Thessalonians 4:9 (HCSB)

In the tapestry of any church, the threads of love have the miraculous ability to weave a harmonious melody that resonates throughout the congregation. Love possesses the unparalleled capacity to mend divisions, inspire acts of service to the less fortunate, ignite fervor for missions and evangelism, and even kindle a passion for financial contributions, nurturing children, adorning nursery walls, or erecting a new sanctuary for the youth. Indeed, love stands as the supreme motivator behind every facet of church action, transcending all boundaries.

Yet, we may find ourselves at times grappling with the realization that our love may not always abound as we desire. What then, in moments when our love feels insufficient?

In 1 Thessalonians 4:9, we are tenderly reminded that our Heavenly Father is the ultimate teacher of love. Love, you see, is not merely a fleeting emotion, but a resolute action that flows from the heart. The sacrificial death of our Lord Jesus Christ upon the cross stands as the pinnacle of love's expression—the most profound act of love ever witnessed. The heartwarming truth is that the same God who sent Jesus to die for us can also impart to us the divine wisdom and capacity to love one another within our neighborhoods and our church communities. Let us be reminded that love possesses the transformative power to revolutionize every aspect of our church life. It is the very essence that breathes life and vitality into our congregation.

Therefore I ask in this sacred moment, to lift your heart in prayer to the Almighty. Humbly seek His divine intervention and implore Him to expand your capacity for love towards those individuals or groups within your church for whom you may not yet feel a deep affection. Remember, love changes everything, and it holds the key to reinvigorating the very life of the church.

May your fervent prayers for increased love be answered abundantly, for it is in the boundless depths of love that we shall witness the restoration, revival, and radiant growth of our beloved church.

Prayer

Consider praying a prayer like this:

Dear God, I do not feel much love for _____ *(you know which name to put in the blank).* I'm asking, and counting on, you to teach me to love _____ the way you love him or her. Thank you for hearing my prayer prayed in Jesus' name. Amen.

Day 16

Be a Peacemaker

"The peacemakers are blessed, for they will be called sons of God." Matthew 5: 9 (HCSB)

In our tumultuous world, where unrest and conflicts often seem to be the prevailing winds, it is undeniable that hate gains a foothold when disputes erupt. In the face of conflict, lines are drawn, and people find themselves divided into opposing camps. In the wake of such discord, trust is shattered, and the repercussions can resonate for years to come.

Remarkably we find that the same tempestuous winds of conflict can sweep through the sacred corridors of the church. Within these hallowed walls, individuals may find themselves taking sides, and disagreements can cast a shadow upon the congregation. It is crucial to recognize that when conflict infiltrates the church, it is the adversary, Satan, who emerges as the sole victor. It becomes apparent that many of the disputes that plague our churches are not rooted in matters of biblical doctrine but rather in personal choices, preferences, styles, and habits.

In the midst of this spiritual battlefield, the teachings of our Lord Jesus Christ shine like a beacon of hope. Jesus imparts the divine wisdom that peacemakers are an essential need within His body, the church. Those endowed with the gift of peacemaking possess the remarkable ability to quell conflicts and foster an environment of tranquility, enabling the church to function in harmonious unity. We must recognize that the actions of a few have the potential to undermine the effectiveness of the entire church within its community.

The divisive forces of conflict within the church have torn families asunder, fractured friendships, and disrupted the peace of neighborhoods. Conflict breeds bondage, while peace bestows the gift of freedom. It becomes evident that the church body must be bathed in the waters of peace in order to flourish and grow.

As members of the church, it's crucial for us to focus on bringing peace to our community. We need to take this responsibility seriously and work towards making our church a calm and harmonious place for everyone. Remember, peace is essential for our freedom and for our church to function well. Let's keep praying to God for guidance as we strive to bring peace to the body of Christ.

Prayer

Ask God to help you identify ways for you to become a peacemaker in your church.

Day 17

Read Mark 10:42-45

> *"And whoever wants to be first among you must be a slave to all."* Mark 10:44 (HCSB)

While attending a conference in Mexicali, I had the honor of meeting a lady who embodied charismatic qualities of Pentecostal holiness and service. As he worked incessantly to help and serve brethren in the conference, he exuded an air of heavenly grace. Even though I could not find her name, her altruistic acts made a lasting impression on everyone who witnessed her. As the faithful worshiped and were cared for, she took center stage as a hospitable servant. She was a genuine conduit of the Spirit because of her captivating personality and her passionate desire to serve.

There are many individuals in the building blocks of modern churches who claim to be leaders, but not all of them have a plan. With its vast assortment of personalities, each with their own distinct qualities, the ecclesiastical landscape is as varied as the sky itself. There are not many people in the world who are as devoted to serving others as the Woman from Mexicali.

The teachings of our Lord Jesus Christ admonish us that many aspire to rule, but we are summoned to a loftier calling, that of "ministers" in the eyes of the King James Version or "servants" in the modern tongue. Finding like-minded people who are willing to help and make a difference in the lives of other believers is essential for bringing about change in the church. Let us not confuse leading with catering to other people's wants and needs as we work to revitalize our church.

The Woman from Mexicali, with a radiant smile that could only be heaven-sent, poured forth blessings upon those she served. In her actions, gratitude found its voice, echoing through the hearts of all who were touched by her benevolence.

Prayer

What ways do you serve others in your church? Pray asking God to show you ways you can serve the Body of Christ through your church. Ask God to give you the best understanding of where to serve in the church. Also pray that your church understands their BEST place to serve as the Hands and Feet of Christ in your community.

Day 18

Begin with Brokenness

Read Nehemiah 1:1-11

> *"When I heard these words, I sat down and wept. I mourned for a number of days, fasting and praying before the God of heaven."* Nehemiah 1:4 (HCSB)

Accepting brokenness is frequently the heavenly catalyst via which God reveals His vision. Nehemiah is a tragic example of a person whose spirit was broken for the sake of a city and its people. Adversaries had ravaged the protective walls of Jerusalem, leaving the city vulnerable and steeped in disgrace. In the midst of this precarious circumstance, Nehemiah sought the spirit of God, freely surrendering to His direction, and making himself accessible for the great purpose that God had in mind.

Courage and unwavering commitment become essential in propagating the gospel. Nehemiah vividly painted a contemporary portrayal of what true service entails.

1. Throughout his life, Nehemiah had an unquenchable hunger for learning. His curiosity extended to the city and its

inhabitants. What inquiries do you need to make about yourself? Is the congregation yearning for a spiritual revival? Are you devoted to spreading the message of Jesus, igniting faith in more hearts? When was the last time you shared the gospel with someone?

2. Nehemiah confronted the unvarnished truth. He discovered that the protective walls were in ruins, placing the people in imminent danger. Are you prepared to confront reality? Your congregation relies on your commitment. Do you lack zeal and fervor? It is imperative for you to experience spiritual rejuvenation as a devoted follower of Christ.

3. Nehemiah took immediate and decisive action. He wept, prayed, fasted, and ultimately surrendered to God's will. What steps do you need to take to inspire gospel-sharing within your congregation? Is it time to surrender, weep, pray, or fast?

Are you experiencing a profound brokenness over the current state of the church to which God has called you?

Prayer

I challenge you to ask questions, accept reality, and act now. God desires to use you as a servant.

Day 19

Be Salt

Read Matthew 5:13-14

> *"You are the salt of the earth. But if the salt should lose its taste, how can it be made salty? It's no longer good for anything but to be thrown out and trampled on by men."* Matthew 5:13 (HCSB)

The incredible power to exert influence is within our reach as devoted followers of Jesus. The power to lead others to justice is in our hands when we use it for good. Matthew 5:16 says that when we give our lives to Christ, our very presence becomes a light that leads others to praise God. Also, it is important to remember that, as Luke 17:1-3 warns, we have the power to turn other people away from God. Having a positive effect on other people for Christ is like being "salt," while having a bad effect on other people is like being "salt that has lost its taste."

Just as a thermostat plays a vital role in regulating temperature during the extremes of warm summers and cold winters, so too are we called to act as spiritual thermostats. When the atmosphere around us becomes spiritually heated, we, like a thermostat, can adjust and work in tandem with the Holy Spirit to bring about a transformation. Our role is not to be passive but to actively influence the spiritual climate.

Consider the analogy of a thermometer placed in the same room. Unlike a thermostat, a thermometer merely reflects the existing temperature of the surroundings. If the room is warm, the thermostat adapts to the prevalent conditions. As the salt of the earth, our calling is higher – we are summoned to influence for the cause of Christ rather than passively conforming to our spiritual surroundings.

In essence, we are called to be dynamic influencers, driven by the Holy Spirit, shaping the spiritual climate around us rather than being shaped by it.

Prayer

Is your daily life and witness more like a thermomcter or a thermostat? Pray that God will give you strength and wisdom to be a good influence for Him.

Day 20

Rely on God's Power

Read 1 Corinthians 4:16-20

"For the kingdom of God is not a matter of talk but of power." 1 Corinthians 4:20 (HCSB)

We say and really believe that Jesus is the rock on which our salvation rests. Still, it is very important to look into what is driving your Christian path. Many different reactions are prompted by this idea. Some say it is because of strong prayer, others say it is because of powerful teaching, and still others say it is because of the constant support of a caring church family. Others might even make the funny suggestion of electricity. Still, there are some people who connect with sources that will never truly help them in their Christian walk. Taking this into account, let us also talk about what keeps you involved in the church. When it comes to your local assembly, what is the driving force behind its remarkable growth and advancement?

There is no doubt in the Bible that the Kingdom of God is more than just words. Words can inspire, but words alone have no lasting value. Someone once said something smart: "Words are cheap."

Our Almighty God's limitless power is one of the things that amazes us. To give our church new life, we need to actively connect with the holy power that comes from God! As excited and committed members of the body, let us consciously draw on the transformative power that God so generously gives us.

To what extent are you utilizing the power that God has given you? The entire Bible is filled with examples of God using supernatural power to provide for His people, and you can be confident that He is still doing so today!

In what ways is your church currently utilizing the power of God? It is God's intention to be the most powerful source of spiritual strength for your congregation. He wants His children to connect with the limitless power of His Word. Are you setting aside time every day to dive into His Word? God wants His children to pray with all their hearts. Are you having honest talks with Him every day and paying close attention to what He has to say? God also wants His children to tell others about the Gospel. Are you busy telling other people about the Good News?

Prayer

Dedicate yourself to praying and reading His Word daily. Commit to inviting ten new people to your church. See how your church responds when you encourage others to do the same. Anointed with divine strength, your church will experience a renaissance.

Day 21

Strengthen Your Faith in the God Who Revives

Read Ezekiel 37:1-14

> *"This is what the Lord God says to these bones: I will cause breath to enter you, and you will live."* Ezekiel 37:5 (HCSB)

The dry bones that were scattered throughout the valley produced an image that evoked two words within the heart of the prophet: a solemn meditation on death and a thundering sense of sorrow. This portrait was painted in the searing embrace of the sun. It was the conclusion that these bones were a depiction of God's own chosen people that weighed even more heavily on the spirit of the prophet than the terrible vision itself. They were already in the grip of death, and their resurrection required nothing less than a supernatural spectacle. They had already given in to death's grasp. Let us keep in mind that our community is in desperate need of a profound touch from the heavens, and let us dedicate every fiber of our souls to assisting in the emergence of such divine intervention.

Despite Ezekiel's unfaltering faith, this otherworldly vision presented a significant obstacle. A question beyond his wildest imagination came from God: *"Son of man, can these bones live again?"* The prophet Ezekiel responded with humility, saying, *"O Lord*

GOD, *you know"* *(v. 3),* His words mirrored his conviction that nothing short of a miracle from God would be required to bring these dried bones back to life, revealing the depth of his thinking.

In this heavenly vision, God accomplished a heavenly operation that was beyond the understanding of man. According to what Ezekiel said, the dead bodies were miraculously brought back to life when their bones fused together and their sinews and flesh enveloped them. Similar to how Israel was revived and revitalized, the dry bones were also reinvigorated.

God takes great pleasure in giving new life to things that seem dead and dying; this is the deep lesson here. Could we pause to consider whether we maintain the same steadfast belief that God can work the same amazing wonders in our lives and within the sacred confines of our church as He did for Ezekiel and the people of Israel?

Prayer

Prayerfully ask God to strengthen your faith as you continue to ask for revival in your relationship with the Lord and in the church meeting.

Worship Beyond the Music

We often equate worship with the familiar sounds of music and singing. While these are undeniably powerful expressions of our adoration for God, they are not the only forms of worship He desires. As we delve into Scripture, we discover a rich tapestry of worship expressions, each as vibrant and meaningful as the next.

In your role as servant leader, it's essential to remember that worship extends far beyond the sanctuary and the music. We are called to cultivate a congregation where worship is a lifestyle, not just a Sunday morning event. Let's consider the traditional image of worship – a grand sanctuary filled with soaring hymns and instrumental harmonies. While undeniably powerful, it's easy to overlook the extraordinary acts of worship that occurred outside these sacred walls.

One might imagine the dedication of the temple as the pinnacle of worship. With its vast choirs, intricate instruments, and ceremonial splendor, it certainly qualifies as a grand spectacle. Yet, as we explore the depths of Scripture, we find that even this magnificent event pales in comparison to the heartfelt expressions of ordinary people.

As motivators, you must inspire your congregation to seek worship experiences that extend beyond the familiar. Consider Paul and Silas, bound in chains and plunged into the depths of despair. Their response? To sing hymns to God. Their worship, born from the crucible of suffering, was a fragrant offering that shook the very foundations of their prison. It was a testament to the indomitable human spirit and the power of praise to transform even the darkest of circumstances.

You can encourage your congregation to find their voices, even in the midst of life's challenges, and to let their worship be a beacon of hope for others.

Or take the anonymous woman who anointed Jesus with costly perfume. Society deemed her unworthy, yet her extravagant act of love and worship was a powerful proclamation of her faith. In a single moment, she overcame shame and fear to offer her most precious possession. Her worship was a fragrant offering, a tangible expression of her deep-rooted devotion.

You must help create a safe and welcoming space where people feel empowered to express their worship freely, without fear of judgment.

The widow's mite, a seemingly insignificant offering, held profound significance in the eyes of God. It was not the amount given, but the depth of sacrifice that captured His attention. This simple act of generosity reveals the transformative power of surrendering your resources to Him.

You can challenge your congregation to consider how their giving reflects their worship and to cultivate a spirit of generosity within your church community.

Abraham's willingness to sacrifice his beloved son, Isaac, is a staggering example of obedience and worship. In this ultimate test of faith, Abraham demonstrated a level of surrender that is both humbling and inspiring. His worship was not expressed through music or words, but through an act of complete trust and obedience.

As a Peacemaker, you must model a life of obedience and surrender to God's will, inspiring your congregation to follow suit.

And finally, we come to the ultimate act of worship – the surrender of Jesus Christ. On the eve of His crucifixion, Jesus prayed, *"Not my will, but Yours be done."* In this moment of profound agony, He offered the perfect sacrifice, a selfless act of love that redeemed humanity. His worship was the ultimate expression of humility, obedience, and love.

You must continually point others to the cross, reminding them of the ultimate sacrifice and calling them to a life of surrender.

As you deepen your own worship experiences, remember that worship is not confined to a particular place or style. It is an outpouring of your heart, a response to the overwhelming love and grace of God. Strive to worship Him not only in your songs and prayers, but also through acts of love, service, and obedience. May your life be living sacrifices, offered wholeheartedly to the One who first loved you.

You have a unique opportunity to shape the worship culture of your congregation. By emphasizing the breadth and depth of worship, You can inspire your people to experience a more profound and meaningful connection with God.

How can you create a worship environment that encourages a variety of expressions?

ROMANS 10:9

Week Four

Day 22

Discern God's Plan

Read Matthew 6:9-15

> *"Your kingdom come. Your will be done on earth as it is in heaven."* Matthew 6:10 (NASB)

In this verse, Jesus shows us how to pray wisely. Each part of His teaching helps us understand more about prayer. God has a perfect plan for our church, and we can see it in Verse 10. In God's amazing kingdom, our church is very important. Through the power of the gospel, God wants His kingdom to spread from our homes and neighborhoods to our cities and the whole world. Our prayers reach heaven when we sincerely ask, "Your kingdom come." We ask God to guide His work in our church so His kingdom can grow and thrive.

When the eyes of the Almighty gaze upon our church, He beholds not only its present state but also its boundless potential. In the mind of God, He envisions a glorious destiny that beckons our church towards a "preferred future." His love for our church knows no bounds, compelling Him to shepherd us towards greater heights. His divine plan unfolds like a tapestry of purpose.

In the fervent utterance of *"Your will be done on earth as it is in heaven,"* we humbly petition God to unveil His divine vision for us. Through the sacred act of prayer, we embark upon a journey of discernment, seeking divine guidance and uncovering the divine "next steps" He has ordained. The most meaningful words we can hear when we try to bring new life to our beloved church are the whispers of God's voice that come through prayer.

Prayer

This day, pray and ask God to show you and the other people in your church what He has in store for the future. Tell Him you are ready to do what He asks. In prayer, ask yourself: Will my skills and gifts help my church carry out the Great Commission?

Day 23

Choose Your Side

Read Joshua 5:13-15

"Neither," He replied. "I have now come as commander of the Lord's army." Then Joshua bowed with his face to the ground in worship and asked Him, "What does my Lord want to say to His servant?" Joshua 5:14 (HCSB)

As Joshua, in preparation for the imminent battle, beheld a formidable figure wielding a drawn sword, his heart naturally led him to approach this enigmatic presence and inquire whether it stood as an ally or adversary. The response from this mysterious being, whom Joshua would soon come to realize was an earthly manifestation of the Almighty Himself (Jesus), resonated with profound significance. The divine reply said that this person was neither on their side nor against it. Instead, it said that this person was the Captain of the Lord's heavenly army. Joshua respectfully bowed down and worshiped this holy being out of awe and respect.

During times of growth in the church, it is all too easy to pick sides, telling the difference between people who seem to back our vision and people who seem to be against it. In spite of this, let us take a higher road that will bring us closer to the Lord. The best way to tell if we are in line with God is by seeing how our hopes for His church match up with His holy plan as written in the Bible. It shows up when we humbly submit to the power and leadership that God has set up. It comes out in our deeds and attitudes, just like Christ's character did.

Therefore, let us pause and reflect, measuring ourselves against the criteria outlined above: Are we truly aligned with God and His divine vision for the church?

Prayer

Today, you might want to pray that God will help you match your goals with His plans for your church. Pray that His will for your congregation and the town where He has put you will show in what you say, do, and how you act.

Day 24

Pursue the Keys to Healing

Read 2 Chronicles 7:12-14

"(If) My people who are called by My name humble themselves, pray and seek My face, and turn from their evil ways, then I will hear from heaven, forgive their sin, and heal their land." 2 Chronicles 7:14 (HCSB)

As the day went on, the air was filled with intense joy and boundless hope. Seven years of hard work went into building the holy Temple, which was then dedicated to the Lord. It was a big deal because God's presence came down in a way that was hard to understand. It was like fire came down from the sky and burned up the sacrifice. The Temple was filled with the glowing glory of the Almighty, which amazed everyone.

In the midst of the silence of the night, God bestowed upon Solomon the presence of His holy presence and bestowed upon him great understanding. During the dedication day, the Lord revealed that not every day would be as magnificent as the day of the dedication. There would be times when, in an eager effort to bring His straying people back into His loving embrace, God would allow droughts and pestilences to demonstrate their commitment. This would be so that they would be

69

more determined to return to Him.

During these hard times, the Almighty told Solomon that His people held the key to renewal. There were four sacred keys that would open this divine restoration: humility, prayer, a sincere desire to see the beautiful face of God through fellowship with His people, and turning away from sin abiding in His Word.

Remember that God's people are His church today. There are discernible signs within many congregations that herald the need for spiritual rebirth and revitalization. Perhaps, your own church finds itself in such a season. The crucial question we must all ponder is this: Are we diligently laboring towards the renewal of our spiritual journey, armed with the sacred keys of humility, prayer, a relentless pursuit to fellowship with His people, and a steadfast abiding in His Word? These keys are essential to releasing the divine spiritual renewal and rebirth that our souls and churches long for.

Prayer

Ask God to help you and others in your church walk with Him in humility, lean on Him through prayer, seek His face in other Christians, and read His word honestly, which will lead to turning away from sins that keep you from being close to Him.

Day 25

Love Jesus above All

Read Revelation 2:1-7

> *"... But I have this against you: you have abandoned the love you had at first."*
> Revelation 2:4 (HCSB)

The closing refrain of one of my most cherished hymns resonates in my heart: "Oh, how I love Jesus, because He first loved me." In the moment that these words emerge from the depths of a heart that is truly honest, they transform into a harmonious symphony of praise that is presented to our most precious Lord. It is not enough for our love for Jesus to only be a melody inside our worship; rather, it ought to serve as the very heartbeat and driving force behind every attempt that we make in His name.

According to initial impressions, the church at Ephesus appeared to be a congregation that was highly valued. It was even the Lord Himself who praised their unrelenting labor, unflinching fortitude, ethical walk, and unwavering adherence to the prescribed doctrine. These efforts were produced out of a sense of commandment keeping rather than an outpouring of genuine love and obligation for their Savior. However, a serious issue overshadowed their excellent activities, the fact that they were born out of commandment keeping. The Christians in Ephesus were on the verge of falling into the abyss without ever being aware of it, which would severely compromise their ability to serve as a beacon of light to the rest of the world.

Despite their best efforts, numerous believers get entangled in a web of legalistic religious obligations and rituals, with little to show for their devotion. In the hustle and bustle of their "hebraic" traditions, they frequently forget about the important duty of cultivating their love for Jesus. A stirring of their very essence, a resurgence of the heart, is what they actually need. Let us heed the loving exhortation of Christ Himself, who beseeches us, *"Remember therefore from where you have fallen; repent, and do the works you did at first. If not, I will come to you and remove your lampstand from its place, unless you repent."* (Revelation 2:5 ESV).

As we introspect, let us each ponder this profound question: Is our love for Jesus the driving force and unwavering motivation behind all our endeavors for His kingdom?

Prayer

Tell Jesus how much you love Him. If needed, repent for allowing your love for Him to grow cold.

Day 26

Seek God First

Read Matthew 6:33

> *"But seek first the kingdom of God and His righteousness, and all these things will be provided for you."* Matthew 6:33 (HCSB)

A glimpse at our bank statement, a perusal of our day planner, a study of our church calendar, or a reflection on our time spent on the Great Commission can often unveil the hidden tapestry of our priorities. Misaligned priorities, when they are allowed to take precedence, have the potential to bring about suffering and disarray into the fabric of our lives, marriages, families, and other places of worship. Nevertheless, our cherished Savior, Jesus Christ, has left behind for those who follow Him a promise that is both profound and conditional. If we, as believers, make the decision to bring the heavenly kingdom of the Father to the forefront of our lives, then we will discover that we are lacking nothing in the magnificent mosaic of creation. This is a promise that is worth so much! Feelings of not having our wants met could be a warning sign that our priorities are no longer in order.

To seek God first is an admission that we are completely dependent on Him, that we need His divine direction very much, and that we are forever committed to His cause. It is very important to understand that this is the best way to get through life and work faithfully in the sacred ministry. We need to look at all of our choices through God's divine lens, whether we are dealing with the daily stresses of life, trying to raise godly children in a world that is becoming less and less godly, catching a glimpse of a new vision for our church, or trying to live happily within our means.

As you think about the beautiful weave of your life, the purity of your marriage, the strength of your family, and the lifeblood of your church, please ask yourself: Are you really seeking God first? What big choices do you need to make right now?

Prayer

Take Jesus' challenge and seek the Father's kingdom first. Ask God to help you see your life, marriage, family, and ministry from His perspective.

Day 27

Consider What Others Think

Read Romans 15:1-3

> *"Each one of us must please his neighbor for his good, to build him up"*. Romans 15:2 (HCSB)

Christians in a church are like family because they all believe in Jesus Christ, the Son of God and our Lord and Savior. Though they are all part of God's family, each soul in the church has its own thoughts and heartfelt wishes. However, we shouldn't forget that these different points of view can lead us astray when they go against the Church's divine goal and vision.

In our collective journey as a church family, we are admonished by the Apostle Paul in Romans 15:2 to seek to please one another. Harmony reigns when we labor together in unity, focusing our energies on the shared goals and purposes set before us, rather than pursuing individual desires in isolation. An act of profound love and care is to inquire of our fellow family members about their aspirations and the underlying reasons behind them. When we approach our church family with a heart of love, considering their needs and desires, we contribute to the establishment of an atmosphere of divine tranquility.

Let us all take a moment for introspection, and ask ourselves: In what meaningful ways are we actively promoting the interests and well-being of our fellow church members? May our love for one another be a beacon that guides us towards greater unity and harmony within the family of God.

Prayer

You might want to pray about it today, asking God to open your ears to the needs and desires of a fellow churchgoer. Pray that God would also grant you the ability to understand their true feelings throughout this discussion.

Day 28

Pursue Church Unity

Read Psalm 133:1-3

> *"How good and pleasant it is when brothers live together in harmony!"* Psalm 133:1 (HCSB)

There aren't many things that are more disappointing and unpleasant than getting into angry arguments with other church members over small things. At times when tempers are high and voices are raised, even small problems can seem very important. But afterward, when relationships are broken and people leave the church because of disagreements about things that were more about personal taste than anything else, these fights leave a bad taste in everyone's mouth.

Now, let's look at the beautiful and peaceful scene that the holy words of Psalm 133 paint. When a community comes together to seek knowledge of and service for God, working together to carry out God's plan and purpose for the church, a truly beautiful scene appears. Not only does it make God happy, but it also gives His people a chance to be a part of a bigger outpouring of the Holy Spirit, which makes their love for the Lord stronger. This togetherness is beautiful to see.

As we embark on our journey of growth and renewal within the church, let us reflect upon the ways in which we are actively nurturing unity among our church family. Are we diligently working to foster an environment where the bonds of unity are strengthened day by day? Moreover, are there fellow members within our church family with whom we sense the need for Christian reconciliation, that the wounds of division may be healed and unity restored in the love of Christ? Let us earnestly seek the Lord's guidance and grace as we navigate this path of unity and growth within the body of Christ.

Prayer

Please pray today that God will help you be a peaceful person in your church. Take into consideration praying that God would bestow upon you a spirit that is able to bring about peace and reconciliation in order to assist your church in its journey toward growth.

The Compliment Plate

As you gather around the family dinner table each night, embark on a sacred tradition. Let there be a special plate, a plate of compliments, gracing your midst. This plate shall serve as a vessel for the outpouring of affirmation and encouragement. Whosoever is bestowed with the honor of the compliment plate for that evening shall receive words of commendation and affirmation from all who share in the meal.

Let us ensure that this plate of compliments does not remain stagnant but rotates, so that each night a different member of the family, even our dear parents, may bask in the warmth of these heartfelt affirmations. In this practice, let us guide our children to offer words of authentic affirmation, transcending mere surface compliments. For, in the consistent observance of this sacred tradition, we instill in our offspring a profound lesson—the ability to see beyond outward appearances, clothing, and such ephemeral matters, and instead, to seek what is edifying and uplifting, in accordance with the unique needs of others. In a world that often seems devoid of kindness, this skill is a beacon of light and hope.

Let us heed the timeless wisdom found in Ephesians 4:29, *"Do not let any unwholesome talk come out of your mouths, but only what is helpful for building others up according to their needs, that it may benefit those who listen."* Through this cherished practice, may we cultivate a spirit of love, affirmation, and encouragement within our homes, a spirit that radiates God's love to the world around us.

Week Five

Day 29

Love Your Leaders, Don't Idolize Them

Read 1 Corinthians 3:3-4

*For whenever someone says, "I'm with Paul,"
and another, "I'm with Apollos," are you not
unspiritual people?"* 1 Corinthians 3:4 (HCSB)

How often have we found ourselves drawn into
comparisons between our current church pastor
and a former one, hearing phrases like, "Bro. so and
so did things differently"? In many instances, such
comparisons prove unproductive, and they place an
unnecessary burden upon the leader whom God has
appointed to shepherd the congregation during this
season. While it is crucial for every member of the
church to honor and respect their pastor, it becomes
an error when we begin to believe that the pastor
alone holds the exclusive source of divine truth.
Indeed, God can communicate with us in various
ways, but we must maintain a profound reverence
for the servant of God and the divine vision
entrusted to them.

The early Christians in Corinth found themselves
ensnared in divisions within the church, stemming
from the multitude of leadership figures whom God
had employed at different times in their
congregation's history. Instead of unity, some
members chose to align themselves with specific

leaders while opposing others. In light of this division, Paul drew their attention to their mistake and exhorted them to put aside their inclinations for carnal favoritism. As we yield ourselves to the Christ-like leadership that God has anointed over us in our present church, we would also do well to acknowledge and honor those who hold leadership positions within God's local church.

In light of these truths, let us ponder this question: What is one meaningful action you can undertake this week to honor and demonstrate your appreciation for your church pastor, leaders or the spiritual overseers appointed by God for this season in your life?

Prayer

Maybe this would be a good day to pray for your pastor. You might consider praying that God will fill them with the Holy Spirit, restoring the joy of their salvation, affirming them in their calling, and refocusing them on the mission at hand.

Day 30

Become a Church Cheerleader

Read Hebrews 10:24-25

> *"And let us be concerned about one another in order to promote love and good works, 25 not staying away from our worship meetings, as some habitually do, but encouraging each other, and all the more as you see the day drawing near."* Hebrews 10:24-25 (HCSB)

The role of a cheerleader extends far beyond the sports arena. It is a calling to stand as unwavering supporters of the team, rallying the fans to action. In the realm of a ballgame, the fervent cheers of the fans can indeed wield a profound influence, propelling their team towards glorious victory. Likewise, in the sanctuary of our church, while each of us assumes a unique role on the team, there are moments when we are called upon to embrace a role akin to that of a fervent fan. Sometimes we find ourselves in the midst of the action, while at other times, we take our place in the stands, passionately cheering for those who toil tirelessly for the noble cause of Christ's mission.

You become cheerleaders for your fellow brethren when we affirm the divine workings within our brothers and sisters who labor in the vineyard of ministry. You stand as fervent supporters of the team when you respond with hearty "amens" to the truths expounded by your pastor. Your voice rises in jubilant praise as you participate joyfully in worship and extend warm greetings to the guests among your church. It is in the exuberant approval of your voice during your church business meetings that you propel the team toward greater ministry accomplishments. In the hallways and gatherings of the congregation, a single individual's positive attitude can ignite a chain reaction, making a tangible difference as they vocalize your unwavering support for the team.

Therefore, let us contemplate the present and future endeavors within the life of the church for which we can offer our resounding vocal support. May your cheers resound as a symphony of encouragement, uplifting your church family in their sacred journey of faith.

Prayer

Pray today that God will show you ways you can support your church vocally with encouraging words as you move toward congregational revitalization.

Day 31

Discover and Do Your Part

Read 1 Corinthians 12:1-7

> *"A demonstration of the Spirit is given to each*
> *person to produce what is beneficial."*
> 1 Corinthians. 12:7 (HCSB)

A church that aspires to embark on a journey towards community renewal must boldly proclaim and accentuate two pivotal truths. These truths serve as the bedrock upon which transformation can be built: firstly, the recognition that every individual possesses a unique role to play, and secondly, the profound understanding that a single person has the potential to enact significant change.

In 1 Corinthians 12, we glean a sacred revelation that underscores the first truth. It teaches us that God, in His infinite wisdom, imparts a distinct spiritual ability to each member of His church. The indwelling of the Holy Spirit when we first believed (Born Again experience) empowers us to serve the body of Christ in invaluable ways. Also the Baptism of the Holy Spirit with evidence of Speaking with tongues has empowered with gifts of power to edify the church. This revelation elucidates the fundamental truth that each one of us holds a vital role within the divine tapestry of the church.

Equally vital is the second truth—emphasizing that one person has the capacity to wield a profound impact. Many among us may grapple with a sense of hopelessness concerning church growth, often believing that the entire congregation must unanimously rally. While congregational unity and engagement are indeed significant, it remains an immutable fact that a solitary individual, aflame with wholehearted devotion to serve God within the local church, can spark an awe-inspiring transformation. Such an individual, fervently witnessing, praying, giving, serving, loving, and living for Christ, becomes an inspirational force, touching the lives of others and, in return, being used and blessed by God in their unwavering faithfulness.

Rather than passively waiting for others to join in, I implore you, dear brethren, to seize this moment. Decide today to be that one person, aflame with the desire to make a difference within your congregation. Will you, in a fresh surrender, consecrate yourself anew to Jesus Christ, with the fervent hope of being used by Him to foster the growth and renewal of your church community?

Prayer

Consider praying today a prayer of re-surrender. Maybe you could offer yourself to God the way you did when you first came to Him. Maybe also you could ask God for personal direction in how to live your Christian service to the fullest in the place where He has put you to serve and grow.

Day 32

Build Up The Church

Read 1 Corinthians 14:6-12

> *"since you are zealous for spiritual gifts, seek to excel in building up the church."*
> 1 Corinthians 14:12 (HCSB)

In these sacred verses, the Apostle Paul addresses the tender souls of Corinth, young Christians seeking to grasp the essence of spiritual gifts. There exists within their hearts a longing to possess these divine endowments. However, Paul tenderly reminds them that these spiritual gifts are bestowed upon us by God for a singular purpose—to edify and strengthen the body of Christ, His Church.

One lamentable challenge that we encounter within the contemporary church is the lack of understanding regarding how to effectively utilize our spiritual gifts to build up the body of Christ. The Scriptures illuminate the profound truth that through the baptism of the Holy Spirit, each believer is graced with at least one spiritual gift from the hand of God.

Now, I implore you, have you diligently sought to discern your spiritual gift(s)?

The second challenge that besets us is the reluctance of individuals to actively seek and employ their divine gifts. When one has experienced the baptism of the Holy Spirit, marked by the evidence of speaking in tongues, and has identified their spiritual gift, a sacred responsibility rests upon their shoulders—to employ these divine endowments for the glory of God and the edification of the church.

It is disheartening that often, in our discussions, we hear pastors testify to the moving of the Holy Spirit in their midst, yet the focus is not sufficiently placed on how Spirit-baptized Christians are actively fortifying and uplifting the church. Indeed, if God has graced us with these gifts, it is His expectation that we put them to use! The church, when its members actively employ their spiritual gifts, should indeed have an abundance of willing workers.

A thriving and growing church is one that harnesses the spiritual gifts of its members, utilizing them to fortify the body of Christ and reach out to the community for the cause of our Lord, Jesus Christ. Let us, with fervent hearts and willing spirits, commit ourselves to this noble endeavor, using our spiritual gifts to their fullest extent, to the glory of God and the advancement of His kingdom.

Prayer

Pray today for God Baptized you in the Holy Spirit and to give you a spiritual gift and how He wants you to use it to build up His church!

Day 33

Love One Another

Read John 13:34-35

*"... I give you a new commandment: love one
another. Just as I have loved you, you must
also love one another."* John 13:34, (HCSB)

In that sacred Upper Room, where the Savior
imparted His final instructions to His apostles, He
chose to commence His discourse with a profound
and enduring commandment—He challenged His
devoted disciples to love one another in the same
manner He had loved them. The deliberate priority
of this directive within the Upper Room underscores
its supreme significance.

Love and unity, my brethren, stand as the very
cornerstone of growth within the church. Jesus
himself declared that the world at large would
identify His disciples not by their eloquence or their
grandeur, but by the depth of their love for one
another. Indeed, there are times when the church
languishes or falters due to the absence of genuine
love among its members, leading to division and
discord. As the world observes, it is uncertain
whether the world can genuinely be reached by a
group of people who do not constantly demonstrate
affection for each other.

In the timeless work of Francis Schaeffer, "The Mark of the Christian".[1] It is eloquently stated that the love of Christ, manifest in the lives of believers, serves as the distinguishing mark setting them apart from the world. Schaeffer astutely concludes that the world possesses a legitimate right to scrutinize the authenticity of Christ's claims as the Messiah, the Savior, and the Son of God, based on the tangible evidence found in the scriptures and lives of His followers.

Can Jesus truly bring about life transformation? Do His disciples lead lives that starkly contrast with the patterns of the world? Do they indeed demonstrate genuine love for one another, even in the most trying of circumstances?

Let us engage in deep introspection. Do our lives bear witness to the unity and love that characterize Christ's disciples? Do our actions and attitudes reflect the transformative love of Jesus? May our existence, permeated with love and unity, serve as an irrefutable testament to the world that Jesus is indeed the One who possesses the power to transform lives and infuse them with His divine love.

---

[1] Schaeffer FA 2013. *The Mark of the Christian*. InterVarsity Press.

Prayer

As you reflect, acknowledge the supreme significance of love and unity within Your local church, pray for guidance and strength to embody these virtues in your daily life. Ask for help to love one another, ask for grace to overcome divisions and discord within your community. Also pray that your actions and attitudes always demonstrate the transformative power of love, even in the most challenging circumstances.

Day 34

Schedule a Church Check-up

Read Acts 11:19-30

"The Lord's hand was with them, and a large number who believed turned to the Lord". Acts 11:21 (HCSB)

Is your life, marriage, family, career, and church thriving in health and vitality? When we look to the church in Antioch, we find a vibrant and robust community, brimming with spiritual health and strength, a testimony to the health of its active members. News of this remarkable church's vitality even reached the distant city of Jerusalem. It is an indisputable truth that people cannot help but talk about the church, whether in praise or critique.

Barnabas, a faithful messenger, bore witness to the *"grace of God"* in action when he arrived in Antioch. This prompts us to consider, what do people observe when they encounter us? As representative of our church, do they witness the "grace of God" powerfully at work through your life?

Are you bringing a proactive and healthful way of life into your cherished church community? A healthy member of the body of Christ exhibits certain traits:

1. **Commitment:** In the same way that

oppression could not stop the early Christians from sharing their faith, a healthy member stays firm in sharing their faith also.

2. **Evangelism:** The church in Antioch centered its discussions around the life-transforming message of Jesus. Do your conversations and actions prioritize the Gospel in your worship and gatherings?

3. **Adaptability:** While the core message of the Gospel remains constant, a healthy church welcomes change in methods as the Lord leads, recognizing that the ways we reach others may evolve.

4. **Collaboration:** Just as Barnabas sought Saul's assistance in teaching the believers in Antioch, healthy church members embrace a collaborative, team-oriented approach to ministry.

5. **Discipleship:** Barnabas and Saul devoted a year to teaching a multitude of believers in Antioch. Healthy churches understand that evangelism and discipleship go hand in hand.

6. **Stewardship:** Tithing and offerings are not merely financial acts but demonstrations of generosity and support for the church's service, outreach, and operational needs. A healthy member practices both with a willing heart and a sense of duty.

7. **Trust:** The Antioch church placed their trust in leaders like Barnabas and Saul.

Submission to church leadership is a hallmark of a healthy member.

As we reflect on these qualities, let us examine our lives and roles within our church community. May we be vibrant vessels of the "grace of God," actively contributing to the spiritual health and vitality of our church, and ultimately, to the glory of our Lord and Savior, Jesus Christ.

Reflection:

Is your church doing well or facing challenges? If it's doing well, how are you maintaining its health? If it's facing challenges, what steps are you taking to address them?

Day 35

See The Power of Agreement

Read Acts 6:1-7

> *So the preaching about God flourished, the number of the disciples in Jerusalem multiplied greatly, and a large group of priests became obedient to the faith"*. Acts 6:7 (HCSB)

In this verse, we are graced with a profound revelation of the transformative power that dwells within the unity and agreement of the saints. As a devoted member of the church, ablaze with the Holy Spirit's fire and zealous for the mission of evangelism, it is incumbent upon us to grasp the profound significance of walking hand in hand with our fellow believers.

When the body of faithful believers aligns their hearts and minds in harmonious accord, a supernatural outpouring of God's grace and power is set into motion. This divine synergy leads to the exponential growth and expansion of our beloved faith community, for our God is a God of multiplication. This sacred principle underscores the irrefutable importance of nurturing an atmosphere of peace, harmony, and unity within the hallowed walls of our church. These elements are the sacred pillars upon which we embark on the sacred journey towards the blessed goal of a spiritually vibrant and healthy church, pulsating with the heartbeat of the Holy Spirit.

In Acts 6:1-7, we encounter a stark contrast in the mindset towards congregational decisions and their divine outcomes. The church, ever in need of divine guidance, sought assistance in ministering to the widows among its faithful congregation. In this hour of need, the godly leadership presented a divine solution, which found favor and resonance within the hearts of the congregation (Acts 6:5). The result was nothing short of miraculous—a unified church, fortified by the heavenly agreement, continued its sacred mission of spreading the Gospel far and wide, tirelessly laboring to bring forth more disciples into the radiant light of Christ's love.

So how can you contribute to this divine symphony of congregational agreement, ensuring that the decisions made within our sacred assembly align with the divine will of our Lord and Savior? Pray fervently, seek the guidance of the Holy Spirit, and let the Word of God be your guiding light. Engage in heartfelt discussions, always seeking the unity of purpose that flows from the throne of heaven. For in unity, we find strength, and in agreement, we experience the manifestation of God's miraculous grace. Let us join hands, hearts, and spirits in the pursuit of congregational harmony, for through it, we shall see the manifestation of God's glory in our midst. Amen and amen!

Pray

Please pray that God will give wisdom to your church leaders regarding a plan for church growth and that their plan will find favor before God and in the congregation.

Integrity, Accountability, and Witness:

Stewardship

Scripture emphasizes stewardship. Many of Jesus' parables deal either directly or indirectly with stewardship issues. Why is stewardship so important? I believe it is because it is an outward visible indicator of an inner spiritual condition. Show me how someone handles their money and material possessions and it tells me volumes about their relationship with God. The same can be said for a couple and the same can be said for church. How a believer deals with financial and material issues speaks loud and clear about their relationship with God and their local church.

In regards to the local church and believers, many words could be used but let's focus on three key words: Integrity, Accountability, and Witness.

1. **INTEGRITY** -Managing money with integrity means being honest, correct, and telling the truth. One way to describe integrity is as the opposite of deceit. When a believer is honest with his money, he does it based on the values, beliefs, and principles they say they follow.
2. **ACCOUNTABILITY** - It is very important. Keep track of how much money comes in, how you save it, and what you use it for. Good

internal rules and a strong relationship are important for an operation. Higher up, it acknowledges that everyone who believes knows that money belongs to God. None of us owns the money the Lord gives us; we are just managers of it. Problems will arise if someone or a group treats money like it belongs to them.

3. **WITNESS** - The way a belivers handle their finances and material possessions will present either a positive or negative witness to the church community. An individual's witness is made stronger or weaker by their reputation. The same is true in the church. Over time a local church and its members get a reputation for how they handle financial issues. That reputation then impacts the church's collective witness to church members and to lost people in the community.

For some, these three words may communicate different concepts but they are in reality very connected. There are three ways of saying a very similar thing. In your church, do all you can to make sure you are a good steward and are faithful. Also set the example, help facilitate, enhance and strengthen others in church to also be faithful.

Week Six

Day 36

Look for God Among You

Read 1 Corinthians 14:24-25

> *"and as a result he will fall facedown and worship God, proclaiming, 'God is really among you.' "* 1 Corinthians 14:25 (HCSB)

What would you say is the most important thing about what you do for your church?

For many people the answer would be: "church meets my spiritual, emotional, or relational needs but I don't do much; I would like to for my church". As you think about your church, who are some of the people that have or are making a difference in your life? What are some of the ministries of your church that deepen your relationship to the Lord? And who is making sure those ministries are active?

When I was a youth pastor, I attended many different churches. I notice some churches are very outward to visitors while others have a harder time approaching strangers. In the text we read today, we find what I think is the best response to the question "What do you say is important to this church?"

First, an unbeliever discovers the truth about a Savior, next accepts Jesus, and finally shouts "God is really among you!" How great if this could be because you are allowing God to use you in your dedication and faithfulness to the local church of Christ. It is easy to look at the devotion of churchgoers and see that God is the center of that church.

Prayer

Pray for God to show you how He is moving in your church. Ask God to help you reflect His presence to a lost world.

Day 37

Obey His Marching Orders

Read Matthew 28:16-20

> *"Then Jesus came near and said to them, 'All authority has been given to Me in heaven and on earth.'"* Matthew 28:18 (HCSB)

In the sacred realms of the spiritual battlefield, when a high-ranking officer issues forth his divine decree, the hearts of the faithful are stirred, and they heed the call with unwavering obedience. Our Supreme Commander, Jesus Christ, has spoken, and His voice reverberates through the halls of heaven, summoning His church to action. The Great Commission is not a mere suggestion or an optional endeavor; it is a divine imperative. Our Lord and Savior expects nothing less than absolute obedience to His divine marching orders.

Our mission begins within the sacred walls of our homes and radiates outward, touching the farthest corners of the earth. The Great Commission serves as the unshakable mission mandate for every congregation, regardless of its form, size, or style. We are all enlisted in this holy crusade, equipped by the Holy Spirit, and empowered by our faith.

In the divine act of going forth, our Lord has not merely called us to record decisions but to engage in the sacred work of making disciples. A disciple, my beloved, is one who passionately pursues knowledge and follows in the footsteps of our beloved Savior, Jesus Christ. Are you intentional about the divine task of disciple-making within the sacred confines of the Church you attend? Have you crafted a sacred strategy for reaching the nations with the life-transforming Gospel? Fear not, for our Supreme Commander promises that we shall never tread the path of the mission field alone; His divine presence is our constant companion, our guiding light, and our source of unwavering strength.

You and I, dear soldiers of the faith, have been summoned to attention and entrusted with a divine assignment that possesses the power to change lives, mend broken marriages, restore families, revive churches, and transform nations. Let us not falter or waver in our resolve; let us obey our Supreme Commander-in-Chief's divine marching orders with unwavering faith and zeal. With the Holy Spirit as our guide and Jesus Christ as our banner, we shall march forward, victorious and triumphant, bringing the light of His love to a world in need. Amen and amen!

Prayer

Reflect on how you've responded to the Great Commission. Have you and your church treated Jesus' command as optional or mandatory? May you allow the Lord to use you to impact the nations for His glory!

Day 38

Check the Temperature

Read Revelation 3:14-22

"So, because you are lukewarm, and neither hot nor cold, I am going to vomit you out of My mouth. Revelation 3:16 (HCSB)

When the unsettling waves of sickness grip us, whether due to a regrettable meal, a winding and treacherous road, or the relentless assault of a contagious virus, we find ourselves in a state of discomfort. Nausea is a distressing sensation. However, there is a deeper and more profound discomfort that we must address—the spiritual nausea that afflicts our Lord and Savior, Jesus Christ.

In scripture, Jesus sent forth a stern challenge to the Laodicean church on numerous fronts. Yet, it was not their external challenges that left Him nauseated; it was the lukewarmness that had crept into their midst. A lukewarm church has the power to turn the stomach of our Lord and make Him sick.

So, what led the once-vibrant Laodicean church to this tepid state? The root of the issue lay in their belief that they were self-sufficient, that they no longer needed Jesus on a day-to-day basis. In their self-reliance, they unwittingly shut the door to their Savior. Jesus, the very heart and soul of the church, found Himself standing outside, knocking on the door of His own sanctuary, hoping to be invited back in.

It is a sobering truth, that many in the church, whether through their deeds or their unspoken attitudes, rely more on their structures, strategies, and human efforts than on the living presence and power of Christ Jesus. Our Redeemer stands, even now, outside the fellowship of many congregations, yearning to be welcomed back into the center of our worship and devotion.

But take heart, for there is hope for lukewarm people. Jesus, in His boundless mercy, extends to His people the opportunity to repent and change their course. He invites us to cast aside our self-sufficiency and to rekindle our dependence on His glorious presence and divine power.

Therefore, let us examine ourselves and the congregations we participate at. Does your church really count on the powerful involvement and presence of Jesus Christ? Take a moment to think about how much you need Him every day. Let's be careful, because the way we act and think as a church can really make Jesus sick.

May we, in humble repentance, open wide the doors

of our hearts and our sanctuaries, inviting our Lord and Savior to once again take His rightful place at the center of our worship, our lives, and our church.

Prayer

Position yourself to discover what Jesus thinks about you. If you and your faith family are nauseating Jesus, hear His knock, open the door, and invite Him in. He longs to fellowship with you!

Day 39

Strengthen What Remains

Read Revelation 3:1-6

> *"Be alert and strengthen what remains, which is about to die, for I have not found your works complete before My God."* Revelation 3:2 (HCSB)

In the divine evaluation of the church at Sardis, our Lord and Savior, Jesus Christ, offered not only His assessment but also a sacred action plan. His words resound with profound wisdom when He urged them to *"Strengthen the things which remain."* It is a clarion call to recognize the areas in which the church was still vibrant and faithful, and to fortify and nurture those aspects before they withered away.

Likewise, in the grand tapestry of the body of believers, each member possesses unique strengths and gifts, bestowed upon them by the divine hand of God. These strengths, like precious gems, are to be recognized, cultivated, and used for the glory of the Kingdom.

Some among us are anointed with a fervor for missions, eagerly embarking on mission trips and generously supporting the global work of the Gospel. They are like shining beacons, lighting the path for others to follow in spreading the love of Christ to the ends of the earth.

Others excel in the sacred ministry of hospitality, radiating the love of Christ by welcoming outsiders with open arms, making them feel cherished and accepted, free from judgment, and enveloped in the warmth of Christian fellowship.

There are those blessed souls whose hearts are attuned to the art of worship, leading congregations into the very presence of God through heartfelt singing and other expressions of adoration. Their voices become vessels through which the Holy Spirit flows, uniting the assembly in divine communion.

Therefore, take a moment to reflect and identify the areas of strength that God has graciously endowed you with. Seek the guidance of the Holy Spirit to discern your unique gifts and talents. Just as Jesus admonished the church at Sardis to strengthen what remained, let us endeavor to nurture and utilize our strengths for the advancement of God's Kingdom and the edification of His body. By doing so, we become faithful stewards of the divine gifts entrusted to us, bringing honor and glory to our Lord and Savior, Jesus Christ.

Prayer

Would you pray today that God would reveal to you and others in your church those areas where your congregation is strong. Ask God to help you build on that area of strength for His glory and the good of the church and the community where God has placed you.

Day 40

Evaluate Your Church

Read Revelation 3:1-6

> *"To the angel of the church in Sardis write: 'The One who has the seven spirits of God and the seven stars says: I know your works; you have a reputation for being alive, but you are dead.'"* Revelation 3:1 (HCSB)

Your church is evaluated every week. The first time guests who visit have an opinion about your church. The senior adults who attend have convictions about the life and ministry of your congregation. The young families have some thoughts as well as the youth. The community in which your church is located also has something that comes to mind when they think of your church.

These opinions are varied and may have some merit. The opinion, or rather judgment, that matters most is the one offered by Jesus, the Head of the church. Jesus has some thoughts concerning your role in the congregation, and the road to spiritual growth begins with seeking Jesus' view of your church.

How does your congregation's perception of your church's effectiveness differ from the perspective of Jesus?

Prayer

Consider praying today that God will help you understand how Jesus views it and what He wishes to see happen for your church to move into new life and ministry and be an influence for Christ in your community.

ABOUT THE AUTHOR

Rev. Ángel Ruiz has been in ministry since 2006 and is currently the pastor of a local congregation, as well as a senior professor at Areopagus Bible College and Seminary in Southern California. In addition to teaching and preaching on a wide range of biblical topics, Rev. Ruiz travels regularly to churches of all sizes to deliver specialized seminars in theology and apologetics. He has served as Dean of Students at Summit Bible College. He has served as District Youth Director at Full Gospel Church of God and Director of Family Ministries at The United Methodist Church. In these roles, he was charged with youth leadership development and day-to-day youth programs that impacted teens. Prior to joining the staff at Hope in Christ Community Church, Rev. Ruiz was assigned as a pastor at San Diego Church of God.

Also from Angel Ruiz:

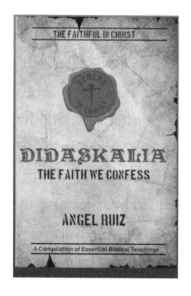

PULLING OFF
THE PETALS

"best way to glorify God is
to say No to Calvinism"

by Angel Ruiz

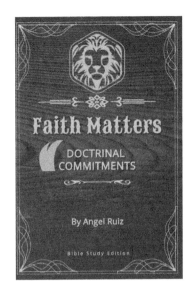

Faith Matters

DOCTRINAL
COMMITMENTS

By Angel Ruiz

Bible Study Edition